My First Book about Giraffes

Amazing Animal Books
Children's Picture Books

By Molly Davidson
Mendon Cottage Books

JD-Biz Publishing

Read More Amazing Animal Books

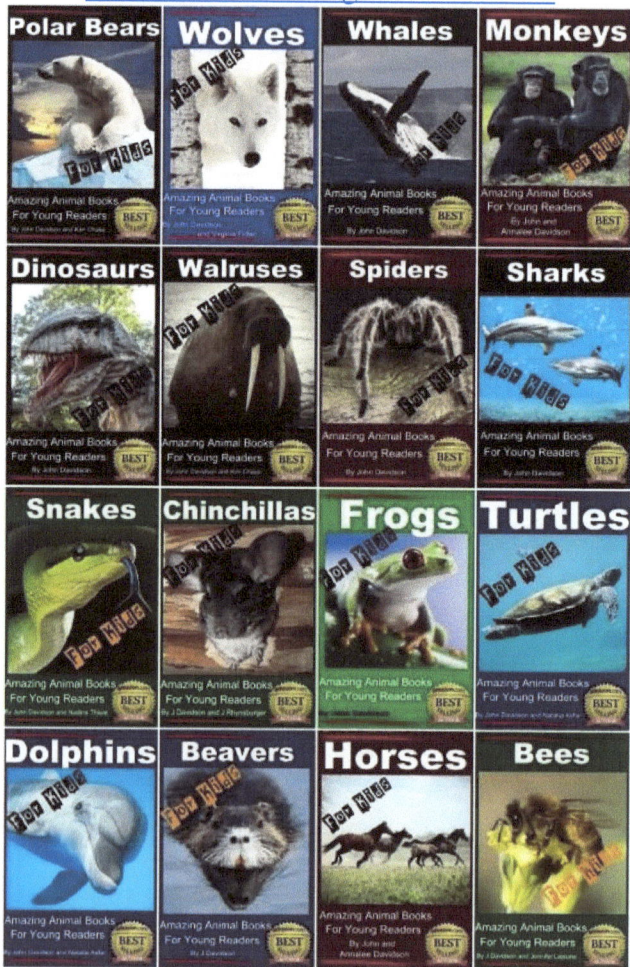

Purchase at Amazon.com

Download Free Books!
http://MendonCottageBooks.com

Table of Contents

Introduction

Giraffes are so adorable looking; people cannot help but love them.

So let's go explore the African Savanna and learn about this amazing animal, the giraffe.

What a Giraffe Looks Like

Giraffes are the tallest mammals on Earth; both their legs and neck are about 6 feet tall each!

Babies stand about 6 feet tall, and then when they grow into an adult giraffe they stand between 16 - 18 feet tall.

A giraffe's tongue is 21 inches long, the inside is pink and turns blue gray outside the mouth to protect it from sunburn while eating.

Giraffe's skin has a spotted pattern; every giraffe has a different pattern.

They have two small horns, called ossicones, on the top of their head, which helps protect them in a fight.

They have the longest tail of any land animal; it is about 3 feet long.

Giraffes weigh about 2,800 pounds, which is the weight of a car!

Where Giraffes Live

Giraffes live in the open land of the African Savanna.

Giraffes travel in herds; sometimes even with other animals.

Other animals like to travel with them because giraffes are so tall and can spot predators from far away.

The main predators of the giraffe are lions, crocodiles, leopards, and hyenas.

They fight predators by kicking them with their strong legs, sometimes it kills the predator.

Giraffes live about 25 years in the wild.

What Giraffes Eat

Giraffes are herbivorous; this means they don't eat meat, just plants and fruits.

They walk long distances to find food, their favorite food is Acacia trees, but they also eat mimosa leaves, wild apricot leaves, twigs, and shoots.

Giraffes spend most of their day eating; they can eat up to 100 pounds of food in one day.

A giraffe uses its sticky tongue to grab leaves from tress. They also use their tongue to clean insects from their face and horns.

How Giraffes Drink

Giraffes drink water only a few times per week, like a camel.

They get most of their water from the plants that they eat.

Giraffes have to spread their front legs open really wide so they can drink. They try to have one giraffe watch for danger because they cannot see very well while drinking.

They can drink up to 12 gallons of water at one time!

How Giraffes Sleep

Giraffes only sleep about 20 minutes total per day.

They take quick 5 minute naps, and do not sleep at night so they can watch out for predators.

They sleep lying down with their feet tucked under their body and their head up.

Giraffes and Their Babies

Baby giraffes, called calves, are in their mother for 15 months before they are born.

The mother gives birth standing up, so the baby falls about 6 feet to the ground bumping its head, which causes it to start breathing.

The calves weigh about 150 pounds when born and they grow 2 inches per day; this doubles their height in one year.

The whole herd helps take of the babies, some will stay and watch the calves while the others go eat, then they switch.

Within 10 hours of being born a baby giraffe can run.

The calves drink their mother's milk for about a year, but they can start eating plants at about 4 months.

Boy calves leave their mothers when they are 15 months, the girls stay until they are 18 months old.

How Giraffes Talk

Giraffes speak at an ultrasonic level, humans cannot them.

Giraffes talk by whistles, roars, moos, and hisses; it all depends on what they are trying to say.

Mothers hiss to their babies when they are going far away from them.

She may also push her baby to safety, to protect it.

If there is danger a giraffe will whistle to warn the herd.

Giraffes also wrap their necks together for two reasons, one when they are mating and two when they are fighting to be leader of the herd.

Types of Giraffes

- **Reticulated giraffe.** Has large spots that are brown, they live in Kenya, Ethiopia, and Somalia.

-**Angolan giraffe.** They also have very large spots and some notches. They live in Angola and Zambia.

-**Kordofan giraffe.** Its spots are smaller and have irregular shapes. It's found in western and southern Sudan and Cameroon.

-**Masai giraffe.** This giraffe has the most unique spots, they look like dark brown leaves. Masai giraffes are from southern Kenya and Tanzania.

-South African giraffe. This giraffe has blotched star spots and lives in South Africa, Namibia, Botswana, Zimbabwe, and Mozambique.

-**Nubian giraffe.** They have lighter brown square spots and live in Sudan and the Congo.

-**Ugandan giraffe.** It is of course found in Uganda and Kenya; it has dark brown, square spots.

-**Thornicroft giraffe.** They live in Zambia and have star and leaf shaped spots.

-**Nigerian giraffe.** The Nigerian giraffe, lives in Nigeria, and is light yellow with red spots.

Please Take Care of Me

Giraffes are hunted for their tails, to make thread and bracelets, their meat, and their beautiful patterned hides.

Some people just kill them as a trophy to hang on their wall.

Humans are also cutting down trees, which is making it harder for giraffes to find food.

Giraffes are not on the endangered list, but we must still be careful so they do not get on the list.

We can stop buying products made with giraffe body parts, do not go on a safari trip to hunt animals, respect their environment, don't pollute, and don't cut down trees.

Come To Visit Me (at the Zoo)

Giraffes are one of the most popular zoo animals, people love them.

Giraffes in the zoo live about 30 years, since they do not have any predators; they also rest more because they are not in danger.

Giraffes eat different foods at the zoo like alfalfa, bananas, grain crackers, apples, and carrots.

Many calves have been born in zoos around the world, and zookeepers take good care of them.

Some Interesting Facts

Boy giraffes are called bulls, girl giraffes are called cows.

Giraffes have high blood pressure; this helps blood to reach their brain.

A giraffe's heart weighs about 20 pounds and pumps around 16 gallons of blood per minute.

The darker the spots, the older the giraffe is.

Their back legs look shorter but they are exactly the same size of the front legs.

A giraffe can run 35 miles per hour.

They can see you in full color, giraffes have excellent eyesight.

Every step of a giraffe is 15 feet long.

Conclusion

We have learned many interesting facts about giraffes, what they eat, how they live, how mothers take care of their calves, and a few interesting facts.

I hope you have enjoyed learning about giraffes.

Website http://AmazingAnimalBooks.com

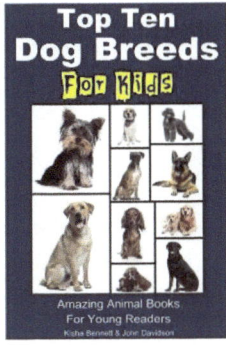

Top Ten Dog Breeds For Kids

Amazing Animal Books For Young Readers

German Shepherds

Dog Books for Kids
K. Bennett

Bulldogs

Dog Books for Kids
K. Bennett

Dachshund

Dog Books for Kids
K. Bennett

Poodles

Dog Books for Kids
K. Bennett

Labrador Retrievers

Dog Books for Kids
K. Bennett

Rottweilers

Dog Books for Kids
K. Bennett

Boxers

Dog Books for Kids
K. Bennett

Golden Retrievers

Dog Books for Kids
K. Bennett

Puppies

Dog Books For Kids

Amazing Animal Books
By John Davidson

Beagles

Dog Books for Kids
K. Bennett

Yorkshire Terriers

Dog Books for Kids
K. Bennett

Dogs Top Ten Dog Breeds For Kids

Amazing Animal Books For Young Readers

Cats For Kids

Amazing Animal Books For Young Readers
K. Bennett & John Davidson

Foxes For Kids

Amazing Animal Books For Young Readers
Zahra Jazeel & John Davidson

Wolves For Kids

Amazing Animal Books For Young Readers
By John Davidson and Virginia Fidler

Our books are available at

1. Amazon.com

2. Barnes and Noble

3. Itunes

4. Kobo

5. Smashwords

6. Google Play Books

Download Free Books!
http://MendonCottageBooks.com

Publisher

JD-Biz Corp

P O Box 374

Mendon, Utah 84325

http://www.jd-biz.com/

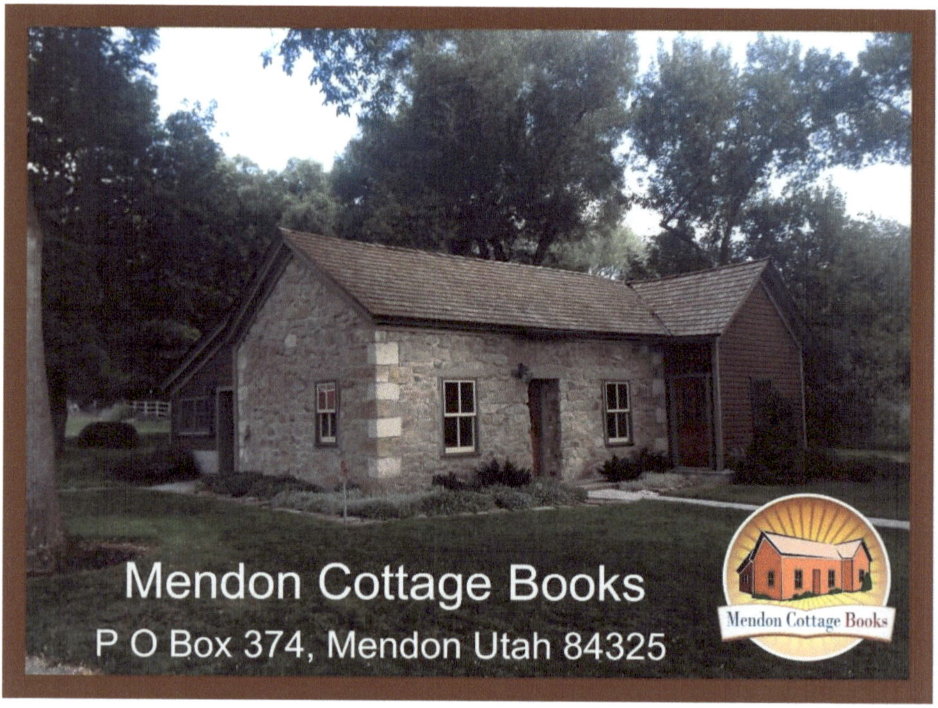

Mendon Cottage Books

P O Box 374, Mendon Utah 84325

www.ingramcontent.com/pod-product-compliance
Lightning Source LLC
Chambersburg PA
CBHW050856290526
45792CB00002B/617